The *Spiritual* Teen:

Awakening to the Real You

ANGELA JAMAL

BALBOA.
PRESS
A DIVISION OF HAY HOUSE

Balboa Press books may be ordered through booksellers or by contacting:

Balboa Press
A Division of Hay House
1663 Liberty Drive
Bloomington, IN 47403
www.balboapress.com
1 (877) 407-4847

Print information available on the last page.

ISBN: 978-1-5043-4900-0 (sc)
ISBN: 978-1-5043-4901-7 (hc)
ISBN: 978-1-5043-4902-4 (e)

Library of Congress Control Number: 2016900466

Balboa Press rev. date: 07/15/2016

To the children who came to and through me:

Zarifa (my daughter from another mother), Kareemah,

Muhammad, Rabia, Kabir, and Omar.

Thank you for allowing me to love other people's children.

I love you.

CONTENTS

FOREWORD

A Spiritual Crisis

Too many young people – of all colors and walks of life – are growing up today unable to handle life in hard places, without hope, without adequate attention, and without steady internal compasses to navigate the morally polluted seas they must face on the journey to adulthood.

—Marian Wright-Edelman

The Measure of Our Success: A Letter to My Children and Yours

Teenagers face great challenges in today's world. We know what they are because we see the issues in our homes, communities, or even in the daily news and on social media. Angela Jamal and I often collaborated in public school settings, helping teens with their problems. In my line of work, some of these may have included stress or more complicated issues with violence at home or neighborhoods, divorces or parental dysfunctions, early pregnancies, and sexually transmitted diseases, along with drugs and alcohol abuse, depression/ anxiety, mental illness, isolation, and lack of adult involvement.

It is the responsibility of every adult—especially parents, educators, and religious leaders—to make sure that children hear what we have learned from the lessons of life and to hear over and over again that we love them and that they are not alone.

—Wright-Edelman

I consider the goal of this book to be an important one. It is the journey of awakening to a very special part of yourself that will allow you to become proactive versus reactive to the dynamics that impact your life. The greatest gift is in helping you believe that you are capable of dealing effectively with life challenges.

Wendy Dunning-Carter, licensed social worker

ACKNOWLEDGMENTS

My mother and father, Amos and Florence Andrews, along with my siblings, Manny, Vron, Val, Trish, (my beloved) Tony—my prayers are with you and your families.

All the wonderful and dynamic teenagers I have had the pleasure of knowing during my thirty-year career in health and physical education.

My South End/Cathedral Projects family, you all know who you are.

Wendy Dunning Carter, thank you for trusting in the process of this book that stayed on the shelf for many years until I felt it was ready to be shared.

Thank you to all of my friends, in-laws, my grandchildren, and most of all, my husband Karam Jamal (1954-2009) our love only had a beginning!

I am forever grateful to all of my student models from Boston Latin, Boston Latin Academy and Boston Public school students that I have had the honor of teaching. Thank you Emma D. for all of your help and of course my cover model, Jazmine with the beautiful face.

A special shout-out to Money and a Dream Entertainment executive "Bir Witness" (my son)—your inspiration in helping me pen my "voice" was truly what made this book come alive.

The New England School of Acupuncture—you nurtured my love for Chinese medicine and healed me for six long years!

Thank you, Dr. Vasant Lad, for my first introduction to Ayurvedic medicine in Boston, and Dr. John Douillard—your work is truly an inspiration to me, and I hope that you are enjoying the Himalayan salt lamp we gave you at Kripalu.

Master Teacher Maharaj Charan Singh, *all* belongs to you.

The Beginning

A great teacher never strives to explain her vision; she simply invites you to stand beside her and see for yourself.

—Dan Millman

Just so you'll know, I have had a lot of great spiritual teachers during my lifetime, and it's not easy trying to present to you what matters most to me without the thought of how they all allowed me to explore the deeper meaning of my purpose in life. Some of this exploration began while in the prime of my health-and-wellness high school teaching career. I would ask myself these questions: Can spirituality be a part of health-and-wellness education for teens? Do teens care about such things? After reading what I'm about to share with you, you may answer my question yourself.

It all began when I attended a presentation with my teenage students, listening to a group of people who were recovering from heroin addiction and sharing their life stories, hoping to help prevent our teen audience from a life of addiction. Each person was from a different economic background and race. After about an hour into the presentation, during questions, one of my high school students made a statement that he had no idea how they could become addicted to drugs and wanted them to give him an answer on why they seemed to have "willingly" ruined their lives. Some of his classmates began to chuckle with admiration for his seeming courage, but I, on the other hand, was a little embarrassed by his nerve to say such a thing purely out of ignorance of the perils of addiction.

But one of the speakers graciously got up and said that it was not a lifelong goal of his to become addicted to heroin. He went on to explain that his addiction was so awful that it felt as though he had lost his soul, and with heartfelt emotion, he again repeated, "It feels as though you've lost your spirit!"

Afterward, the whole room became completely silent. I sensed that all, including myself, were in awe with this powerful and emotionally charged statement. I knew in my heart that this was a profound moment for all of us. I wondered if my students knew what he meant? So, when I returned to class, we began our discussions and writings on this thing called "spirit." That was eighteen years ago, and to this day, I still share this story and continue to discuss and collect the writings of teens on spirituality and what it means for them and, of course, what it means for me. Thank you for allowing me to share with you, the reader, a journey.

With love,

Ms. Jamal

INTRODUCTION

Spiritual Seeking for Teens: Are You Ready?

You are a spiritual being that goes beyond your race, gender, religion, country and even your culture. Recognize this part of yourself and it will allow you to see all of humanity as One.

—Ms. Jamal

Why this book? Even some of my friends and colleagues would say to me, "Spiritual seeking for teens? They're not ready for it! Just leave them alone to be self serving know it all's and temporarily insane members of society until adulthood!" All jokes aside, even if this is true about some teenagers, I say that you are ready. And I will do my best to share with you the ways in which you can become open and available to what is already within you. Allow me to share with you some ideas about spirituality, it's meaning for me, and how you could begin to think about this part of yourself during your teen years. I want to introduce the concept of spirituality as an inner exploration and a way of helping you attain a sense of well-being throughout your life. I also wanted to validate other teens who are discovering who and what they are, without feeling weird, crazy, or abnormal. As a meditator and yoga practitioner since the age of fifteen—and I won't say how long ago that was, even though I will not apologize for any wisdom acquired so far—I realized that to allow myself to be truly content in the world, I had to include a connection with spirit, so why would I not include this as valuable information for any teenager who will be open to it? I am here to say that it has taken a lot of courage and time for me to present my thoughts and experiences to you, so as you read this book and it appears that you have acquired *more* questions about this thing called "spirit" and what role it plays in your life, then I have served my purpose.

Now don't go talking back or arguing with your parents over all of this. Maybe you were raised without religion, or you were raised as a Christian, Jew, Muslim, Hindu, or a Buddhist, and at some point in time naturally question your beliefs and practices for whatever reason. Maybe you described yourself as a spiritual person but were and still are turned off by organized religion. Or you are happy with the religion that you practice and are open to finding the real truth in them. Congratulations! You don't lack faith, as some would believe. To question, to want truth, or to be totally confused about all of this is exactly what I call a "spiritual quest." It will affect everything that you say and do during your lifetime. This book will only affirm you on this positive journey.

I will only, through this book, support your desire toward recognizing the true love that is inside you called "spirit" and to help you discover how powerful it really is!

I do not claim to have all the answers, but if you are sincere and keep open to what I am sharing, I guarantee it will be worth it. Trust me. Been there! Done that! Still do!

CHAPTER 1

The Spiritual Teen: Awakening to the Real You

*Look inside yourself, see what you find, it could be
something that you kept buried for a very long time.
My friend, bring your buried treasure to the surface
of your life.*

—Ms. Jamal, age eighteen, 1974

What is spirit? If you tell me that you have to think a little
about it before you answer, or that you don't know, I would
say, "Good answer!" Now we can begin our exploration. Let's
begin with religion. I am not judging or referring to a particular
system of faith and worship. Do you ever feel rebellious or
misguided about religion? Teens like yourself may be raised
as Christian, Jewish, Muslim, Hindu, Sikh, and the like. At
some point in time, you may question or even challenge these
religious systems. Your parents, teachers, clergy, and leaders
may say to you, "After everything we taught you, you still
challenge, question, or have doubts." Real spiritual seeking
begins with questions. Here's my first question to you: Who
are you, the real you? I have heard it all. "I am my father's son;
I am American, Asian, Baptist, atheist," and so on. Okay, but

I'm here to tell you that you are spirit. You are a loving spirit. You are a spiritual being living in a human body. Explore this concept for yourself, when you are ready. In the meantime, keep practicing how to be a better human being, through acts of kindness and love.

I am here to tell you that you're not just your body, mind, emotions, race, gender, religion, or culture. The real you is the most authentic, loving, and peaceful part of you. Are you surprised? Don't be. Including spirit along with your human qualities helps develop an appreciation of yourself. Read my lips. Oops! Never mind. Read my words: "Spirit is love, and love is what you are." If you're not convinced yet, I'm glad. I've yet to meet a teenager who hasn't challenged this statement, even my own children. They are grown up now and they have found ways to nurture their own spirit, through daily spiritual practices.

Here's something else to ponder. Religion may give you glimpses of the spirit through daily rituals, reading of childhood parables, and acquiring family values and moral laws by which to live. Maybe you're satisfied with those religious practices, and that's all right. But in all honesty, knowing of the spirit has nothing to do with them. A loving essence is found within you, regardless of what you think, what religion you are or are not, where you're from, how much money or education you have, or what country you are from. Get my point? Let me continue; spirit is one, and you're a part of that One. Your spiritual self is divine, regardless of your age, race, culture, or social status. The divine essence that you are is described as pure love, and it exists in all things, so why not include yourself? Celebrate it; pay attention to it. You can even throw a party for it! Just kidding. You get the point.

CHAPTER 2

Discovery of the Spirit

How can I help you discover your spiritual self? The discovery is a very personal and intimate one. It is only experienced inside you. But first, you have to ask yourself more questions— important questions.

Who are you? Where did you come from? What is your life purpose? Now hold on. You may be thinking that this is all too deep. But in order for you to begin to explore this part of yourself, you must keep asking these types of questions. Trust me; you'll receive the most loving answers through great teachers showing up for you. All of life will show up to help you to find the answers to these questions. As you interact within your environment, all forms of social media and the friends you associate with, all help you explore things to satisfy all your desires. All these things inhibit your tendency toward getting answers right away, but guess what—it's normal to not let spiritual seeking be your focus 24/7. You can begin now to develop moments when you can find comfort with my ideas. I'm here to tell you that when you look at life events through the eyes of spirit, it will help you to remember there is more to you than all your mistakes. Are you thinking, *All right, you say that I'm a spiritual being, so who created spirit?* Well, let me put it this way. For something to be created, it must have a creator. This creator, as you may already know, some call God, Jehovah, Allah, Divine Energy, Divine Love, The Force, Light, Love, and so on. But it's more than any name given to it. It's who you are. I prefer to call it Divine Love, but whatever you decide to call it is your decision; no arguments here. Once discovery of the spirit begins, inner peace follows, and you'll realize that you were never and will never be alone.

Paying Attention to Spirit

How do you pay attention to spirit? Your attention will have to be through a practice of silencing and the stilling of your mind. Have you ever tried to stop your mind from thinking about anything? You can begin by reading inspiring books about the experiences of others who have done it. Don't worry; it's okay if this sounds difficult, because we really cannot keep the mind from thinking. You can, however, learn to observe how your mind works and not pay too much attention to all the things it says, especially the negative self-talk that it brings up. Just keep trusting a much more quiet voice within. Listen for a voice that validates the most loving parts of you, not a voice of hurting yourself or punishing or placing shame on you. Try harder to listen to the voice of love within you. It is there, just practice giving it some focus and attention.

Maybe this is where you think that I sound too airy-fairy or that all of what I am saying is just too good to be true. That's okay. Just keep reading. Your feelings and emotions will change from day to day about this, but the nature of your loving spirit is consistent and unchanging.

As you awaken to what I have shared with you so far, you may wonder if there are other teenagers like yourself with serious questions and opinions around spirituality. I want you to know that there are plenty of teens who have already asked questions and received answers that they can live with for now. On the following pages, I share with you some conversations, questions, and answers teens have found for themselves. Throughout the book, I leave spaces for you to include your own thoughts as you contemplate what you have read and what I have shared. This journey of exploration and discovering yourself as a spiritual teen won't cost you anything. Let's just say the spiritual party's on me! The rest will be your own private matter.

CHAPTER 3

*Questions and Answers
on Spirituality for
and by Teens*

Spirituality cannot be taught; it's something very personal that you can experience for yourself. You may give spirit a name—Soul, Light, God, Universe, or even Nothingness—but each of us has to define who we are and what we believe to be spiritual according to our own understanding.

—Ms. Jamal

How do you define Spirituality or this thing called Spirit or Soul?

I look around and see things that are happening in the world and I get confused, but sometimes when I am with someone that I love and I feel a feeling of peace and love that seems so pure, as if nothing else can compare to it. That is spiritual. (Val, age seventeen)

For me, I think that it is important to be in tune with your spirit, it helps you focus, relax, and reexamine yourself. Spirituality is like my chi. (Zhou, age eighteen)

I think spirituality is having a certain peace throughout life. I'm not extremely religious, but I do believe in a creator. With that belief, I get peace and comfort when things get too hard. (Tony, age fifteen)

What do you believe about spirit or soul?

> If I really think about it, the mind is very powerful, and it needs to be powered by a superior. Therefore, I believe I have soul/spirit. (Kareem, age fifteen)

> The soul is the part of us that is pure, like our better selves. I also believe in reincarnation. (Zack, age eighteen)

> I believe that I have spirit that keeps me connected to the earth and other creatures. (Jules, age fifteen)

> I believe that the spirit is the most important. It is the only part that can never be taken away from you, because it is yours. It's deep in your heart. (Catherine, age sixteen)

> I believe spirituality is like a phenomenon. It's inside everyone. It doesn't come to you; you come to it! I believe it takes a lot of dedication, patience, and faith to connect to your spirit. (Ira, age seventeen)

I don't know what spirit is; I never have. But I don't believe that I will always not have an understanding of what I think my spirit is. I know I have one, but I just can't define it. I think it's better at least to admit I don't know. Understanding comes with time. (Sarita, age fifteen)

I believe that I have a soul and that the soul and spirituality is the basis for living. I think our souls are to guide us and to do right in our lives. Without our souls, we could not go on. (Yvette, age fifteen)

Yes, I do believe I have a spirit and a soul. I think of a spirit as the way I act and how happy I am. My soul is the thing inside of me that makes me be alive. I believe that we are too complex to have been created from one cell that divided. We are a miracle or a creation from someone greater, God. Our body is too complex to be scientific. Scientists do not know what makes one live. We are just a pile of dead cells without our souls. Our souls are the life in our bodies. We are here on earth to fulfill something in our lives, to make the best of ourselves, to see if one can find in life the thing that fulfills him or her most. Souls will go to heaven, where the next life will be determined by God, but it's forgotten when we are born to try to figure it out again. (Angel, age eighteen)

SPACE FOR YOU:

I believe that I have a driving force inside me, a soul, something that gives me life. I believe that there is something much greater than money, power, material goods that I'm living for. (Jackney, age eighteen)

I do not believe that a spirit/soul, God, and religion play large roles in my life. Who can say for sure if there is a God or a soul? Religion is blind faith in a powerful being created by people in order to feel less afraid, lost, confused, etc. Everything can be explained scientifically, and no one can confirm or explain the absolute existence of a God or the existence of a soul. These things are the creation of the human imagination. I came from combination of my parents' chromosomes. I don't believe in reincarnation or God creating my soul. As to where I'm going, only time will tell. I think death is nothingness or the absence of everything. (Wadih age sixteen)

I believe everyone has a spirit. For example, when someone says "you're deep," I see it as having something that is deeper than your mind. Spirit is something that cannot be described but can be shown through writings, personality, and attitude. (Saraliz, age sixteen)

I believe that I have a soul and that the soul and spirituality is the basis for living. I believe in God, but I am not very big on religion. I believe that God created all of the things in the world. God gave me free will and the right to choose. God also gave us a soul. I think our soul is to guide us and to do right in our lives. Without our soul we could not go on. (Kenny, age seventeen)

I define myself as laid back and very connected. I'm laid back because I don't stress. I just let fate take its course. Whatever will be, will be. I'm connected because I take time to listen to what my soul is telling me. That's how most of my poems get written. I write what I feel and nothing else. (Keith, age sixteen)

I have faith that there is something higher or something beyond life—for example, God, heaven, angels. I believe that our soul is something that is part of each of us. When it comes to the end, the only thing that matters to me is faith. It's better to have faith than no faith at all. (Anonymous, age sixteen)

I have a soul, and I believe strongly in spirituality. I pray often, and I know or think there must be a higher force than us. And in your life you must have faith, or without it, you are sheltered and inexperienced in real life. I feel I am a great and special person with different qualities. I also feel that everything happens for a purpose and eventually leads to our destinies. That is why I try to be the best person I can be. (Simone, age sixteen)

What do you believe about religion?   What do you believe about spirit?

I was raised without a religion imposed on me. My mother, ironically, grew up religious, but now she hates religion. I believe in a higher power. (Rocky, age eighteen)

Two years ago I was confirmed into the Episcopal Church and thus renewed my faith in God. I made this decision. When confirmed I was asked what I feared the most, and I answered, "Death." (Susan, age eighteen)

I converted to a different religion once the leader of my old church did a sermon condemning gay teens. (Sam, age eighteen)

I don't believe in souls or God, but I do believe that religion is important, not as a reminder to God, but as a reminder of our own mortality. (Paulette, age fifteen)

I believe that there is a God. I believe that God gave me everything I have. Throughout my entire life, He and He alone has given all ideas about science. God gives all emotions, feelings, characteristics, and ideal to us. The bottom line, to me, is that God is eternal. (Israel, age eighteen)

I'm not going to pick a religion just because I was brought up with it. I do feel that everyone has a job or purpose in his or her life. (Omari, age thirteen)

I don't really know what my church believes God's purpose is, but I think God looks forward to the unity of people, and his purpose is for people to come together, and have a connection. (Solomon, Age fifteen)

Religion seems to help people live right. Well, that's what my dad says. (Muhammad age seventeen)

I'm not so sure anymore if I believe this. (Seth, age fourteen)

If a person goes to church because he/she is forced to, then he/she will do things without any regard for the church. If a person goes to church because it really helps them in their everyday life, then religion is worth it. (Sal, age seventeen)

I believe that the spirit is the most important part. It is the only part that can never be taken from you, because it is yours. It's deep in your heart. (Imani age sixteen)

I believe that there's a higher power. ... We are more than just bodies. I don't believe in any certain god. I believe there is a reason we are on this earth. I believe every one of us has a goal we must achieve that will improve society. Humans are more than what we learn of in anatomy, more than bones, cells, and blood. If we were only that, what would be the point of anything? Friendships? Learning? Feeling? I used to be a Catholic, but I don't label myself anymore. It's not fair to put limits on love. I love my life. I love this world and want to improve it. That is why I am here. There are parts of my religion I agree with and parts I disagree with, parts I believe in, parts I don't believe in. I cannot prove that there is a higher power or a soul, but I believe that there must be a reason we are here. There would be no reason to wake up tomorrow. I believe that we make mistakes because we are not perfect, but we are born innocent and good-willed. (Cooper, age fifteen)

SPIRITUAL SEEKING BEGINS WITH YOUR QUESTIONS

I have so many questions about spirituality and religion that sometimes makes people at my church think that I have no faith. This is not the case at all. I love my church and God, but I don't believe in everything that is taught. My love for the spirit keeps me searching for meaning. (Felix, age eighteen)

I don't really know what my church believes the creator's purpose is, but I think it looks forward to the unity of people, and his purpose is for people to come together and have a connection. (Kenya, age fifteen)

Religion might help you in a situation, and it might not. For instance, if you really feel that you are close to God, that He is the one who's making all your decisions for you, you might feel that you don't have to stress, because whatever is the best path for you, God will lead you through. However, if a person goes to church because he/she is forced to, then he/she will do what he/she pleases and might not think twice about religion. (Steve, age sixteen)

Religion is not the most important part of my life. I was brought up in a household that has let me choose what I want to believe in. My parents did not force me into religion; they let me decide for myself. As I grow older, I still don't know what is out there. I do feel that people have souls, but their souls are what they make it. You make yourself who you are. (Jacob, age fifteen)

I don't believe in a name "God," but I believe in a higher power, something that created us and watches over us. I believe it is important to think this, because when times get hard, you can always turn to "it" and know "he'll" keep safe, and that's comforting to know.

I do believe in one's spirit, and I feel that one must fulfill it to know that you have a purpose. I believe in reincarnation, and I think I came from another life, another time, another place. I believe people are put on earth to benefit humanity and will eventually die but be reincarnated to another life to help someone else. I believe I am part of a superior whole. My body is just a shell, but my "soul" is the living part of me, and my job is to fulfill it. (Aisha, age fifteen)

Religion seems to help people live right. Well, that's what my mom says. I'm not so sure anymore if I believe this. (Alson, age fifteen)

To me, spirituality does not have to be connected to a religion. In fact, I see a spirit as who you are. If you were to take away the body, you would be left with a spirit. It is who you are on the inside, thus, you make your own spirit. (Lowell, age eighteen)

SPACE FOR YOU:

CHAPTER FOUR

Mindful Practices for Better Living

Benefits of a Mindful Practice

Mindfulness, in simple terms, means being aware of your feelings, mood and thoughts while in the present moment. When practicing mindfulness, it will allow you to also be more accepting of yourself. For example, I learned about this through a yoga practice. It will not only help you approach life from a calmer, relaxed place, but also help you develop a stronger, more flexible body as well as a more positive self image. I was first introduced to yoga back in the early 1970s at the age of fifteen while visiting my local YWCA. I have loved and reaped the benefits of a yoga practice for years. Back then, unlike today, yoga classes for most young people in the city were nonexistent. I was the only teenager in the class! Some adults would even tell me that I was too young to be stressed. Now, as most of you know, teenagers are just as stressed out as anyone else. Your stressors may not be the same issues as adults, but in this high-pressure, more violent, competitive world of ours, managing stress may still be a problem for you. Today I see an upsurge of young people more willing to embrace a yoga practice. Allow me to introduce my experience of yoga, and let's dispel some of the possible misconceptions you may have.

Yoga may not make all of the problems and stresses in your life go away, but it may just help you learn to be proactive than reactive to them.

–Ms. Jamal

First of all, yoga is not a religion, but it is a practice to develop awareness of the calm and peaceful part of yourself, all while performing physical body stretches or postures called asanas, helping improve muscle strength, increase flexibility and master deep-relaxation nasal breathing techniques. Its origins are from the East (Not East Boston! Excuse my sarcasm.) and many different types of yoga have been practiced by some people for thousands of years. Here in the United States, yoga has been proven through scientific research over and over again to be very beneficial for stress and ways to relax—not only triggering a greater relaxation response in the nervous system, but also improving the health and wellbeing of so many people, young and old. In my experience, a yoga practice may help you develop a more positive body image too. In most yoga studios, there are no mirrors on the walls, so you won't feel the need to look for any of your so-called flaws or how fat or skinny you look. Most of all, you don't have to compare yourself to anyone else. Who cares whether or not you can twist yourself into a pretzel like the next person? For a more mindful practice, I tell the teens to make every effort to lovingly keep their attention on the breathing techniques that I share in the book and allow all other thoughts and feelings to come and go, all the while breathing slowly in and slowly out. This, in turn, helps to maintain your focus on the moment. Staying in the moment is something that all of us need to do. In the moment, self-criticism or anxieties about the past or the future have no place. I understand that your worries may sometimes overwhelm you, but during yoga, forget them and store them until your yoga practice is done. Is this easy to do? No, but one day it will be as you practice being in the moment over and over again. Yoga is a very selfish practice for teens. It's all about *you* and how you feel on the inside and accepting how your body can adjust and sometimes be challenged on the outside with each posture that is introduced to you. Try and make your yoga practice one of your life skills. Being able to go through difficult times, all the while feeling that you could bravely and lovingly embrace one moment at a time, is what mindfulness is all about! As you begin this practice, it may help you cope with many stressful issues. Mindfully take a deep breath in and then slowly exhaling can be a good beginning place to help you relax and just stop and become present. This focused inhalation and exhalation may help you eliminate other thoughts and keep you in the moment. Nasal breathing (breathing through your nose), according to Dr. John Douillard in his book *Body, Mind, and Sport*, shares that the benefits of nasal breathing warms and moisturizes the air headed for the lungs, helping to maintain a proper balance and immunity, which may prevent colds and mucous build up. As you breathe deeper into the lower lobes of your lungs, you are sending a message to your nervous system that all is well. Just imagine sitting quietly and closing your eyes and concentrating on your breath. It will work wonders for decreasing your day-to-day stress levels and overthinking. Try a yoga class in your neighborhood, school or local recreation center. You may also try the relaxation techniques below and on the following pages.

1. Positive Relaxation Technique

Sit cross-legged, keep your head and your back straight, relax your shoulders while inhaling slowly and exhaling slowly through your nose. As you inhale, just focus on the breath as you breathe in and out. You may want to place one hand on your abdomen, to feel it expand during your inhale and contract as you exhale. Just keep breathing in and out and soon you will notice how calm you may feel. This calmness comes as you let go of worries and just trust yourself to just breathe.

There are no worries in the present moment.

You can practice this while lying down or sitting cross-legged with your spine straight and your shoulders relaxed. Place the palm of your hand on your abdomen and, as you inhale slowly, feel the outward expansion of your abdomen, while on your slow exhalation, feel the abdomen get flat again. This can be a very relaxing breathing technique to calm your nervous system. For a mind/body experience, I recommend a positive thought with a slow, deep, inhaling breath and letting go of any worries on your full exhalation.

2. Single-Nostril Breath

Close off your left nostril on your nose with your left thumb and breathe deeply through your right nostril, in and out. Focus only on the breath and relax. Let go of any worries. Focus only on the inhale and the exhale. This focus will help you to feel calm and after you feel relaxed for a minute or so, switch to the other nostril.

Here are a few comments from teens who developed a mindful practice for themselves.

> Personally I am really enjoying my yoga practice so far. It's a great change from the regular gym/school routine. (Mike, age seventeen)

> One thing that I really noticed is that for the first time practicing yoga, I forgot all the stress of school. I think it helped me focus better. I think it's relaxing, and I never have done anything like it before. (Jennifer, age eighteen)

> Yoga helped me to forget my school stress and focus on myself. (Susan, age sixteen)

Yoga helped my breathing improve and helps me to relax, and I use the yoga stretches before I run. (Tina, age seventeen)

During this time in yoga, I've noticed that I have become more flexible in both my thinking and my body. (Calvin, age sixteen)

I think yoga is kind of weird, but it helps me a lot with how I deal with stress. Yoga doesn't just teach you about the exercises and deep breathing. It teaches me how to deal with things a lot better. (Emily, age fourteen)

Journal Writing for Self-Reflection/ Thoughtful Affirmations

You are like a plant that needs watering to stay alive.

Thinking good thoughts about you, speaking pleasant

words to and for yourself, are like watering a thirsty

plant. These are steps you can take and must as often

as possible to affirm yourself.

—Iyanla Vanzant

Journal writing can be a positive way to express your self emotionally and mindfully. You may use a journal as an outlet for you to write about ideas and learn to express or handle confusing thoughts and feelings. As you begin to write about or express what's on your mind in your journal, it will bring clarity and understanding to you as an observer of your written thoughts. Being able to sort through different emotions, no matter what they are, is an important remedy for self-reflection and spiritual nurturing. Just know that journal writing is suppose to be a practical tool for cultivating awareness of your thoughts and feelings. This is another mindful practice. Writing may not seem like a fun thing to do for some, especially if it's something you're not used to doing outside of schoolwork. Begin to approach your journal as a nonjudgmental piece of work only belonging to you and no one else. You can decide if you want to share it. Keeping a journal allows you to be yourself and become your own "best friend."

Write in your journal every day. If you prefer using your computer to type the words and save them in a private folder or flash drive, that's fine too. Just put some time aside to do it and write about anything you want to. Include positive thoughts about yourself, friends, and family, and write about important decisions you need to make. Copy a favorite poem; share your wishes, dreams, and goals with your journal. Anything goes!

As you continue to write in your journal, return to your words days or weeks later and see if some of the issues, feelings, or decisions you wrote about are repeated or resolved, especially if it was something that made you angry or sad. Writing also has a way of allowing you to let go of some negative feelings. Be careful not to dwell on problems or negative issues. Seek a way out of them by writing and asking for help from someone you trust to suggest some positive options or solutions. A journal will reveal so many things to you and may help you make positive changes within yourself. Affirm or support and encourage yourself each day in your journal. Whenever you can, begin your journal with a positive statement or what I call an affirmation. Affirming something good about yourself on a daily basis can be very empowering compared to your constant thoughts of feeling alone in the world or a part of you that brings in the negative self talk at times. You have a choice in what part of you that you want to listen to.

Begin your journal today! Get started by using the next few pages in this book. Here's a few favorite statements or affirmations for and by other teenagers. As you continue, use them or make up a few of your own.

Thoughtful Affirmations:

Today I will tell myself that everything is all right with me!

Today I will forgive someone, including myself.

Today I am grateful to be alive!

Today I will thank someone for being my friend.

Today I will like myself more and criticize myself less.

Journal Entry For You:

Diet/Nutrition Suggestions Made Easy

Tree Pose: Nourish my body and soul

When you allow food to become your medicine to nourish and heal you physically, mentally and emotionally. Then your food choices will change for the better.

— Ms. Jamal

We cannot talk about being mindful just mentally or emotionally, without including the kind of foods that you put into your physical body. Your food choices are influenced by your family culture, religion, parent's income, advertisements, cost, and, obviously, your taste buds. I don't know if you noticed that most food commercials and establishments that serve high-fat foods and high-sugar-based cereals are geared toward young people. There is so much information and factual proof about diet and its relationship to disease. Keep yourself up-to-date on them. Type 2 diabetes and unhealthy weight gain among today's teenagers has risen due to a diet high in sugar, hormone-filled red meats, and, of course, too little exercise. During your teen years, learning to make changes or evaluating the kind of eating habits you have is a good way to begin. Making improvements in your food choices increases your chances of not having to make major changes when you get older. Eating a variety of nutritious foods is the key to a happier lifestyle. You can live on "junk food" but only for so long! Here are some ideas to consider: Enjoy your food without distractions; don't talk on the phone, text, or watch TV. Don't eat when you are emotionally upset either. I know. I know, all these don'ts! Trust me: all of this will get easier, believe it or not. I guarantee that your body will thank you, because your food will begin to digest better, preventing stomachaches and digestive issues for you. You want your foods to be nourishing, not to take the place for your boredom or emotional meltdowns.

Read and learn more about the benefits of whole foods, green-plant foods, vegetarian diets, and foods from all cultures that are healthy and good for you.

Try to eat a variety of nature's natural foods every day. Remember, there are no totally bad foods, just bad choices we make with food. Always mindfully practice gratitude for the opportunity to have enough to eat and nourish your body every day. Take a moment to appreciate having enough food to eat, not to place any guilty feelings on you, but honestly, as some of your parents reminded you, in some parts of the world, clean water and food is difficult to come by, so be thankful! This thankfulness will nurture your gratitude muscle a little more. Remember, gratitude is a Mindful practice that helps nurture a deeper part of you.

In his book *Perfect Health for Kids,* Dr. John Douillard's suggests drinking pure water to stay fully hydrated, as it will support your immune system, increase your strength and vitality, improve your physical and athletic performance, and decrease your susceptibility to illness. The juices and other high-sugar drinks can supply you with a certain level of hydration but may be doing you more harm than good. He also mentions in his book pure water helps with digestion and the important breaking down of fats and proteins in your body as needed (pg.109). Too many of the juices available at the stores have concentrated sugars that affect your blood sugar levels, dramatically affecting your mood and energy levels. I think white bread and white sugars can be substituted with whole grain, such as whole-grain cereals, crackers, and breads. Remember balance is the key for any good nutrition program that you set for yourself. Try and make small changes by reading and educating yourself about good nutrition.

For some of you, this may not matter to you right now, and I am not telling you to "give up" your sweet and low-nutrient foods. It's okay—no judging here. But remember: moderation of low-nutrient foods and an increase in high-nutrient foods are the keys. Supplementing with wholefood vitamins and minerals is a must. As you take my word, I recommend the book *Dead Doctors Don't Lie.* Google it! Learning to make small, gradual changes as needed is the best way. You might want to begin evaluating the kind of diet that you already have. I usually suggest a twenty-four-hour diet recall. For example, make a list of everything you eat and drink for a day. Review it and add a vegetable or delete a high-sugar, low-nutrient food (i.e., trade a candy bar for a high-protein energy bar).

Include fruits and vegetables along with protein foods in your diet. If you want to try some vegetarian food plans, Tofu, legumes/beans, nuts, seeds, tempeh, and other organic soy products are good for additional sources of protein, vitamins, and minerals to add to a vegetarian teen diet. Don't misuse food to try and obtain the so-called "perfect" body. Improving your body image is an *inside* job. Don't let this world tell you the type of body that you should have.

Before beginning any change in your diet, speak with your doctor and nutritionist, especially in regards to losing or gaining weight. There are so many false claims for some weight-loss programs for adults, never mind for the overweight teen. Develop a regular exercise routine at least three times a week. Choose an activity that is *fun* and makes you feel good. The no-pain, no-gain concept is an old one. Exercise is not a punishment—it is something to enjoy and feel good about. Feeling stress-free is how exercise should be done, because then you're more than likely continue it for a lifetime. Your knowledge of these exercise and nutrition tips empowers you to becoming an advocate for your body, mind, and spirit.

Last, but not least, remember to get enough sleep. Healing and rejuvenation take place while you sleep. Begin to fall asleep without the computer or T.V. on, so you can quiet the activity of your mind for a better sleep.

I also suggest that you read or 'google' the benefits of eating organically grown foods, plant based proteins and healthy fats. Check out vegetarian style cooking if you haven't already. At least in our American culture, animals are slaughtered and made to suffer to satisfy our desire for meat. One day out of the week that you go vegetarian can save the life of an animal too. That's just my little "plug" for animal rights. Enjoy foods from all cultures that are healthy and good for you, because making better choices about what you put in your body should begin now and become a lifelong healthy practice.

Angela Jamal

On this page below, I have listed different types of vegetarians for your own curiosity, or if your vegetarian friends come over to hang out with you, you'll have some idea what to offer them. Not to insult your intelligence, but not all vegetarians are just into salads or rabbit food as some teens may tease about! Enough with the jokes, I'll stop now.

Classification of Vegetarians

Lacto-ovo vegetarian: Abstains from eating animal foods and products that contain them, with the exception to eggs and dairy foods

Lacto vegetarian: Abstains from eating eggs and all animal foods and products that contain them, with the exception of dairy products

Vegan: Abstains from eating all animal foods, eggs, and dairy foods and products that contain them

Space for You: *Today I will choose a food as medicine for my body.*

Breakfast:

Lunch:

Dinner:

Snacks:

★Tai Ji Symbol: Supreme Ultimate Potential

If there is light in the Soul

There will be beauty in the person

If there is beauty in the person

There will be harmony in the house

If there is harmony in the house

There will be order in the nation

If there is order in the nation

There will be Peace in the world

Chinese Proverb

CHAPTER FIVE

*How to Achieve Harmony
and Balance during
Your Teen Years*

Seeking harmony and balance must come from inside through honest, sincere, day-by-day living and nurturing of your spirit. Achieving harmony and balance through a relationship with your spirit is possible. Throughout this book, I have shared with you the stories of teens who are doing their best to develop relationships with their real selves. Seeing yourself as a spiritual being is a process that can begin now and will continue on. When you are balanced and in harmony, you will make better decisions concerning your own life. You will begin to feel happier inside; it will show on your face and in your actions.

Warrior Pose: I balance my life with strength and courage.

True balance has nothing to do with the things on the outside of us. Balance comes from a quiet and happier place within us.

—Ms. Jamal

Practicing a life of harmony and balance requires that you try to meet your duties and responsibilities in life. Relax and allow adulthood to come naturally; don't rush yourself into growing up too fast. There are plenty of adults who are not awakened to their spiritual selves and are not making a conscious effort toward spirit. You can begin now during these teen years and enter adulthood with more understanding of your spiritual self. Become more forgiving of yourself and others. Always recognize your value even when others do not. Do charitable and good deeds. All this will help you to strive for a more balanced life each and every day. Keep an open mind and heart to the changes that occur in the world and be a part of that change for the better. Cultivate more divine love into the world. It all begins with you—the real you who knows that there is love within you. You will see this same love within everyone else. Drugs and alcohol have no place in seeking a life of harmony; they will just make you forget the problems of the world for a moment or supply false gratification for an instant and may bring you further and further away from acquiring true balance. Observing yourself is important. For example, try a simple exercise of thinking about your actions and your response to different situations. What you do, whether good or bad, always has a way of coming back to you. This is so you won't make the same mistakes over and over again.

Mistakes will be made, but remember that you are not your mistakes. Remember that each day really is a time for you to work on yourself. You can begin to search for harmony and balance, as long as you establish an attitude and belief that it is possible. Sincerity and patience will get you to your goal. Try to become aware of any positive changes within yourself and continue them. Decide what type of person you want to be, despite any negative thought or deeds that you have done. Acknowledge the love that you have inside and remember that it does exist within everyone.

Teens Share Their Secrets to Achieving Harmony and Balance

My family gives me the strength to keep my life balanced. My parents always talk with me about school, they help me with my homework, and they work so I can have money in my pocket. I also get enough sleep on most nights. Usually I got to bed from 10:30 p.m. and sleep till about 6:30 a.m. This helps me in school. I balance my life between school, friends, sports, and family. (Tom, age thirteen)

I really admire my family, especially my mother. My mother raised my brothers and me all by herself. I learned from her never give up, no matter what you have gone through. (Sophie, age thirteen)

My life is very hectic. There is so much going on; it is considerably difficult to main my sanity. One of the things that I like to do, which is very helpful, is read. I read many type of books, but most are science fiction or about WWII or Vietnam. I also find that it helps to take a day off now and then. (Susa, age fifteen)

Whenever I'm lonely or upset about something, I talk to my friends. They talk to me and often cheer me up. Since they are my age, they understand more. I think to be balanced you need love and support from people. My parents have supported me through life. Balance also comes from my high self-esteem. (Gloria, age eighteen)

I believe that the Creator has provided me with the Holy Spirit, and he is the creator of the world. My world revolves around this belief. I believe that he created me and that I'm here to serve him. This keeps me up. He is always there for me. When everything is down, he is there. He listens. He responds in weird or miraculous ways. He comforts me. It is really nice to know that someone is always there for you whenever you need him, even at 4:00 a.m. Basically, the Creator is the foundation to my well-being. (Samad, age fifteen)

Being balanced to me is doing well in school and eating a well-balanced diet. On good days, my goal for being balanced is getting enough sleep, trying hard in school, and eating/exercising correctly. I try to eat three healthy meals a day, and I either walk or play basketball to stay in shape. I also try to concentrate on my schoolwork. I wish that I could get more sleep, because I realize sleep is very important for me to stay balanced. (Mickey, age sixteen)

I keep my life in balance by talking it over with a person whenever I have a problem. The people I usually talk to the most are my parents, because I know they will give me the best advice possible. They are wise. Whenever I'm angry, I try to do recreational activities such as basketball or play video games. When I play basketball or play video games, it helps me relieve some of my stress, instead of beating up on others. In my life, I try to do the right things. I don't let anyone put me down. I concentrate on goals I set for myself. (Jacob, age sixteen)

I believe that finding the balance within your heart is very difficult. Balance to me is finding and putting all the aspects of your life on a side where you are happy. Balancing school, relationships, and parents can get very stressful. Maintaining a good balance is difficult. For me, balance is something I'm still in search of. Writing poetry is one of the ways I try to stay sane. Writing brings out the emotions that I hide inside. If I'm angry, I get violent. I would punch doors, walls, or anyone that frustrates me. My education is very important to me, and I believe my grades are very connected to my parents' happiness. Once my grades are good, they will be happy, and then it will relieve the five thousand tons of stress. Stress also comes from my relationship. From day one, it has been a major roller coaster ride. One day I'm sad and completely depressed and in tears; the next day, I could be happy and laughing. My relationship has a big effect on my emotions, and it is clearly visible on my face and by my body language. (Kevin, age seventeen)

To keep myself in balance, I write. This is a way of expressing my feelings of love, anger, sadness, or whatever! Sometimes I share my writings with people and if they enjoy them I feel good. I had a wonderful experience last summer at UMass Boston. It really changed my life and changed the way I deal with problems. Whenever I need to think about things, I go to UMass Harbor, and while I am there, I collect my thoughts and prepare to live in the world again. Talking to my best friend also helps. She is the one person I can say anything to the one person I can vent to and the one I can totally be my "goofy, obnoxious" self with. She never judges me, and accepts my flaws, and forgives my mistakes. Whenever I've had a bad day, she can help me feel better. (Asia, age sixteen)

When I begin to feel unbalanced or overwhelmed, that's when God comes in. I listen to some gospel music and everything becomes clear. (Stephanie, age thirteen)

My serenity is gospel music. While listening to positive gospel music, I tend to cry, but they are happy tears.

Something about the music shakes whatever is disturbing me. This keeps me balanced. (Jacob, age fourteen)

I keep myself balanced by writing poems when I'm upset and do not want to keep everything inside. Poetry allows me to express my feelings, and it helps me express my emotions. I also talk to my best friend about my feelings, and finally, I keep a journal. I write down my feelings and things that happen, and that lets me get them out of my system. There are many different ways and ideas that you can use to stay balanced; you just need to find the ones that suit you and use them. (Talia, age fifteen)

CHAPTER SIX

Life Questions
and Answers

Development/Pressures

Why does life have to be so complicated?

> There are so many reasons why, but your attitude plays
> a big part in how you handle complicated matters.
> Keeping balance is a day-to-day practice.

How do I concentrate my attention when I have so many things
to do?

> Make a list of the most important to the least important.
> Take ten minutes to sit calmly and just breathe.
> Affirm yourself first and then do one thing at a time;
> multitasking is so overrated!

Approaching Spirituality

I'm always bored. Is this all there is in life?

> Not according to those who have a spiritual practice.
> You have a spiritual essence—your true self. Explore

this loving part of yourself; it goes deeper than anything ever known.

What is spirituality all about?

Understanding the real you, what you already possess, something no one can take or give you. A God-given beauty and awareness that is within you twenty-four hours a day.

How does one find true peace?

Establishing a connection or awareness of your true self through love.

Why should I care about spiritual matters?

You're right! Why should you? In previous chapters, I revealed some reasons that other teens share.

Does spirituality have any role in real life?

Ask others and see how they answer. Then ask yourself and let your life give you the answer.

Is spirituality a need for everyone?

After reading this book, I hope you have an answer for yourself.

How do I know there is more than the physical?

In reality, we are given signs every moment—dreams, thoughts, emotions, feelings, intuition. They cannot be touched, but we know that they are inside of us.

How do I know there is more than the physical?

Through inner exploration... Yes, tangible things— things that we can touch, feel, taste, smell—are easier to understand, but what about dreams, gut feelings, emotions, we can't see them but we know they are there—unseen senses.

Where do I fit in with all this? Others may think I'm crazy.

A lot of spiritual seekers may think at times that they are crazy. This is a new concept, especially in the western part of the world. You are being bombarded and entertained by social media. Caring about a spiritual practice may be a very new concept for you or others around you. It's time to wake up to recognize that you are spirit in a body, more than a body with a spirit. Take the time to search for answers to your questions. Trust your most loving intuition.

Religion

Why do religions differ so much from each other if there is just one God?

Not only do religions seem to differ, we also give so many names to God! But why not look for the similarity of religions? True religion teaches that we are all one with love. Let love be your focus. The love belongs in all religions.

Do animals and plants have a spirit?

> Every living thing—the ones we see and don't see very
> well, have a spirit.

What is consciousness?

> In the big picture, consciousness is who you are! In the
> small picture, it is the quality of the spirit that either
> awakens little by little or stays asleep to itself.

Why is the mind considered such a problem?

> Don't see it as a problem! Just think of it like a monkey
> before it reaches his destination and finds a banana. It
> swings from one emotion to another. Like a river, it
> keeps riding along with thoughts that never seem to
> end, and like an ocean, its desires run deep and wide.
> When you know the nature of the mind, it is easy to
> learn to observe its littleness compared to your stronger
> loving spirit.

How do I control my mind?

> You don't. Just be more aware and get to know what it is and what it does, and then, once you see that, ask, *Who is doing the seeing? Who is doing the observing who is observing this mind? That is the one who 'controls' the mind.*

Why do I find it hard to control my temper?

> You're not alone on that one. Everyone experiences anger, but by nurturing your loving side, anger will naturally be less, and you will channel it into righteous anger. If you notice, I said "channel" not get rid of it. For example, being angry over seeing someone getting bullied or hurt or wronged may cause you to be angry, but you may help the person. Angry over not getting what you want and hurting someone must be channeled by exercise, deep breathing or just stopping and thinking before you act.

God

Is there a God?

> Is there? Only your experience can answer that for you and mine for me. Is there love? If yes, then to me there is a God—they are the same.

Where is spirit?

> Within you.

Can we ever escape from this high-tech, performance-pressured society?

> Your love within you is a great place to hide sometimes!

Spiritual Teacher

What is a spiritual teacher?

> A teacher of the spirit, it can be man or woman of any race or religion. He or she is someone who has

"mastered" the knowing of spirit. A teacher who may share a path to awaken you to your self.

Why should I do what some spiritual teacher, religious teacher, or anyone else tells me to do?

You're right—why should you? Just begin to open your heart and listen at least and then make up your own mind.

How do I know that a spiritual teacher is the genuine article?

You won't. Your own spirit will let you know. So you may have to practice what he or she shares with you and see for yourself if the teacher is genuine.

Why are only some people "called" to spirituality?

Love calls everyone, but each has a time to go and a choice to answer the "call" as you say.

How important is faith?

> Very important in the beginning of your spiritual journey, but then experience must replace it to stay on track.

What is grace?

> It is what is given to the spirit from the moment it awakens.

Energy

What is the spiritual energy?

> Energy, life force, Tao, melody, formless, love.

Can it really be proved?

> Yes, by those who have experienced and awakened to it.

What do I gain from going to religious and spiritual meeting places?

> Some say that they get comfort from the atmosphere, others get moral support and encouragement to keep them inspired, and some get out to socialize.

Ways of Life

Will I have to change my life to follow a spiritual path?

> Changing your attitude toward life and what your purpose in life may change.

Why shouldn't we eat meat?

> Different people have different reasons. There are political reasons; killing is a moral reason, some say. When we love more, we consider other beings and their right to live.

My friends ask me why I'm vegetarian. What should I say to them?

> Well, if you don't know, then ask yourself why you are. You have to have a reason. Your parents made you, you don't like meat, or you have compassion for and understand the suffering of animals being killed for food.

What is wrong with drinking alcohol?

> Wrong or right is not the question for some, but alcohol changes how your mind thinks—well, only temporarily. Why not deal with thinking clearly?

I won't have any friends or social life if I don't drink alcohol.

> Who says? True friends respect your decision about drinking, and there are plenty of young people around who don't drink too. I know teens that attend alcohol-free parties, but then I know some that pretend to

drink, by holding empty bottles, just to fit in. Which one do you want to be?

Why is the talk of sex and teens such a "touchy" (excuse the pun) subject? Can I have sex and still explore topics of a spiritual nature?

The talk of sex as you describe doesn't have to be, if done with respect, and factual information for teens to make informative decisions around it. Let me put it this way: Sex is not only a physical feeling, but for most, it is also involves emotional feelings. Sometimes these feeling are confusing or complicated. Spiritual seeking may play a part in your decisions if you allow it to. That depends on your values and beliefs. What beliefs do you have about it? Your physical and emotional self has to deal with the consequences of your sexual choices. If you don't have any values of your own, then start establishing healthy values, through education and healthy boundaries for yourself around sexual issues before you decide to do anything.

Is it okay to have a girlfriend/boyfriend and still be spiritual?

It all depends on your culture and belief system around issues with dating. Every teen I have encountered has a different cultural belief, different parental rules that they have to follow, and so on around dating. Cultivating a more loving and kind part of yourself first will allow you to treat someone else the same way, if you do date.

Can spiritual teens still enjoy themselves?

Yes, you can be happy. I know this stuff may seem deep, but nobody said you have to be serious all the time. Loving and recognizing yourself as a spiritual being, allows you to happily connect with the real and most loving part of you.

Helping Others

What is the point of helping others in need when I am going through stuff?

It helps you to get out of your own problems and helping someone else less fortunate than yourself. It will also exercise your "gratitude" muscle, when you feel sorry for yourself and then meet a friend or stranger who is suffering more than you. That's when some teens use the term: "I'm blessed" or "Thank you".

What are different ways to help others?

Helping others is a way of helping yourself, believe it or not...Finding some encouraging words, (even if you find that you don't feel as encouraging to yourself) and giving of your time to help out in any productive and safe way that you can is the first and most valuable service to others.

Will I have to grow up faster as a spiritual seeking teenager?

No, spirit lovingly awaits.

BIBLIOGRAPHY

Douillard, John. *Body, Mind, and Sport: The Mind-Body Guide to Lifelong Health, Fitness, and Your Personal Best.* New York: Three River Press, 2001.

Douillard, John. *Perfect Health for Kids: Ten Ayurvedic Health Secrets Every Parent Must Know.* Berkeley: North Atlantic Books, 2004.

Edelman-Wright, Marian. *The Measure of Our Success: A Letter to My Children and Yours.* New York: Harper Collins Publisher, 1999.

Millman, Dan. *Sacred Journey of the Peaceful Warrior.* Tiburon: HJ Kramer, 1991.

Vanzant, Iyanla. *One Day My Soul Just Opened Up.* New York: Simon & Schuster, 1998.

Printed in the United States
By Bookmasters